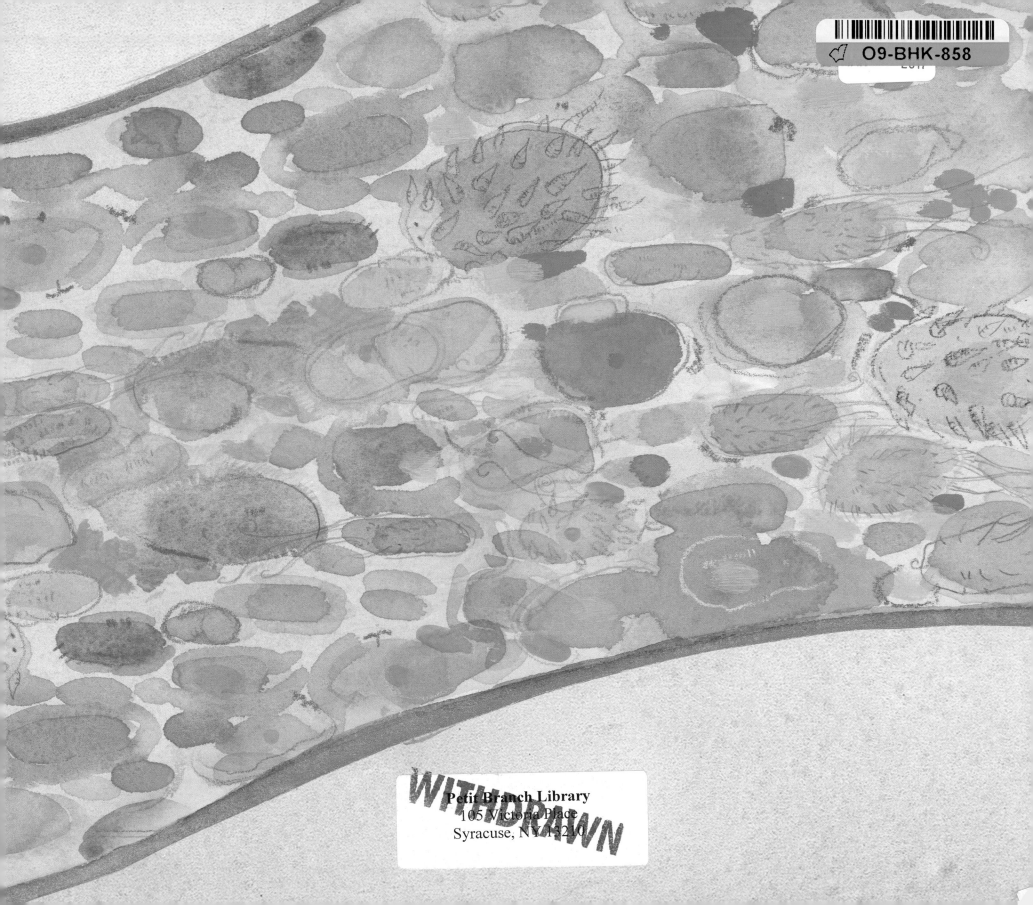

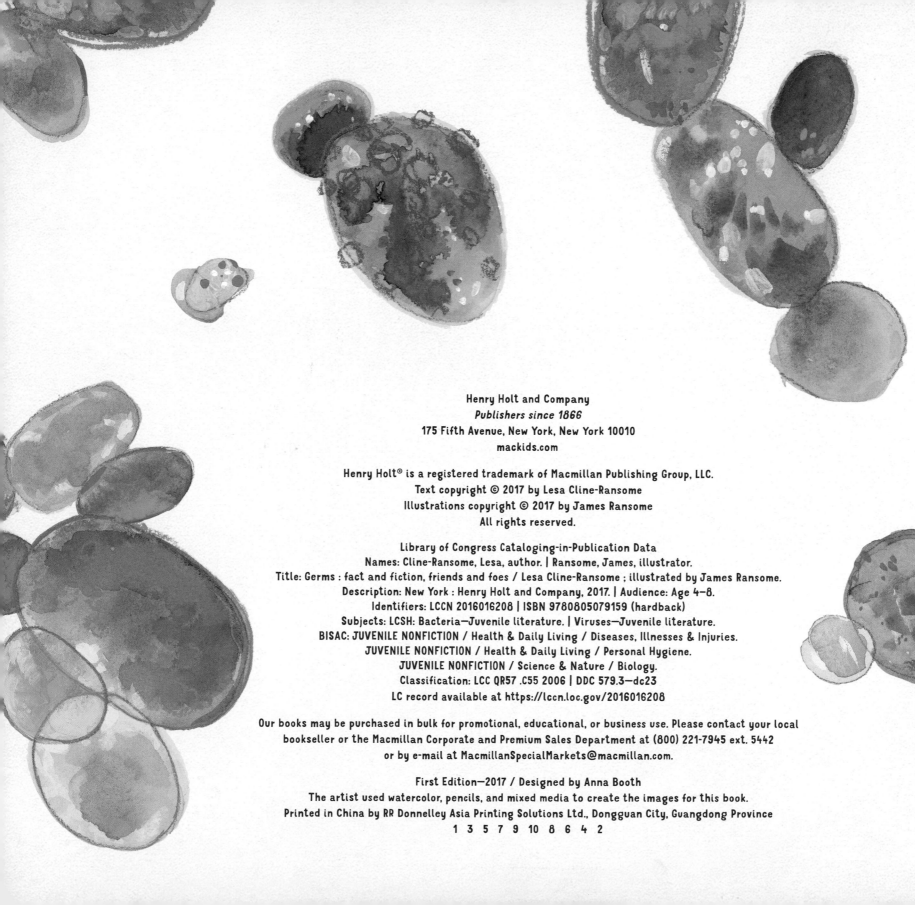

Henry Holt and Company
Publishers since 1866
175 Fifth Avenue, New York, New York 10010
mackids.com

Library of Congress Cataloging-in-Publication Data
Names: Cline-Ransome, Lesa, author. | Ransome, James, illustrator.
Title: Germs : fact and fiction, friends and foes / Lesa Cline-Ransome ; illustrated by James Ransome.
Description: New York : Henry Holt and Company, 2017. | Audience: Age 4–8.
Identifiers: LCCN 2016016208 | ISBN 9780805079159 (hardback)
Subjects: LCSH: Bacteria—Juvenile literature. | Viruses—Juvenile literature.
BISAC: JUVENILE NONFICTION / Health & Daily Living / Diseases, Illnesses & Injuries.
JUVENILE NONFICTION / Health & Daily Living / Personal Hygiene.
JUVENILE NONFICTION / Science & Nature / Biology.
Classification: LCC QR57 .C55 2006 | DDC 579.3—dc23
LC record available at https://lccn.loc.gov/2016016208

Our books may be purchased in bulk for promotional, educational, or business use. Please contact your local
bookseller or the Macmillan Corporate and Premium Sales Department at (800) 221-7945 ext. 5442
or by e-mail at MacmillanSpecialMarkets@macmillan.com.

First Edition—2017 / Designed by Anna Booth
The artist used watercolor, pencils, and mixed media to create the images for this book.
Printed in China by RR Donnelley Asia Printing Solutions Ltd., Dongguan City, Guangdong Province
1 3 5 7 9 10 8 6 4 2

GERMS

FACT and FICTION, FRIENDS and FOES

Lesa Cline-Ransome

ILLUSTRATED BY
James Ransome

Christy Ottaviano Books
Henry Holt and Company • NEW YORK

A long time ago,
before your parents existed,
and their parents too,

before computers and TV—
we were born.

We roamed the earth with dinosaurs.

Later, we stood at the foot of the pyramids . . .

and sailed the oceans with Christopher Columbus.
The first Thanksgiving?
You guessed it—we were there.

Let me introduce myself.

I was born **Salmonella**

(but only my mom calls me that).

My friends call me **Sam.**

I come from a large extended family of a billion or so germs, each of us so tiny, a thousand could spread out on the tip of a pencil and you'd still never spot us. We roam from one end of the world to the other. I have uncles in Europe, aunts in Australia, a sister in South America.

Family reunions are tough. We can never get together at the same time.

As a hardworking family, we spend our days going places many wouldn't dare—between toes, in armpits, around gums and teeth, and inside your ears! It may not always be pretty, but for us it's home.

Our names can get confusing.
We are more often called

E. coli, streptococcus, staphylococcus, yeast, and mold,

but you can call us GERMS.

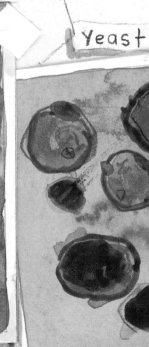

Yeast

E. coli

teriophage

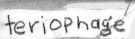

We were once a **powerful dynasty** ruling over everyone we met.

We kept ourselves busy,
but no one knew we existed.
That is, until 1673—when a
Dutch amateur scientist named
ANTONI VAN LEEUWENHOEK
found us through his simple microscope.
Our lives were changed forever.
Now the entire world could see us.

But it was another scientist, **LOUIS PASTEUR** from France, who named us and made us famous. It's hard to believe people once thought unhealthy blood and evil spirits caused illnesses.

Pasteur changed what people believed when he proved that germs were responsible for causing milk to sour, noses to run, and stomachs to ache. He and other scientists revealed our part in causing ear infections, cavities, chicken pox, pimples, and bad breath.

Throughout the world, members of my family were heated until they vanished, injected through needles—never to be heard from again—and killed quickly with medicine. Pasteurization, vaccinations, and penicillin: we called these *poison*. Entire portions of my family were destroyed. But all anyone seemed to care about was the number of **HUMAN** lives being saved.

We've survived, but it hasn't been easy. There was once a time when we could depend on people not brushing their teeth or washing their hands. An entire population of us could live

under just one dirty fingernail.

Over the years, things have changed—hand washing, bleach, rubber gloves, antibacterial this and antibacterial that, and even face masks? Just surviving the day has become a full-time job!

DID I MENTION WE LOVE TO TRAVEL?

We often ride piggyback on fleas, ticks, and mosquitoes, or as passengers in taxis, trains, buses, and boats all over the world.

One good cough and we sail through the air.

Don't get the wrong idea about us.

We germs are not all horrible creatures, just spreading disease and causing a stink. There are really only a few relatives (distant cousins on my father's side) that cause problems and make the rest of us look bad.

There was a time when bad germs built their reputations on fear. They were given colorful names like

YELLOW FEVER,
BLACK DEATH,
and **SCARLET FEVER.**

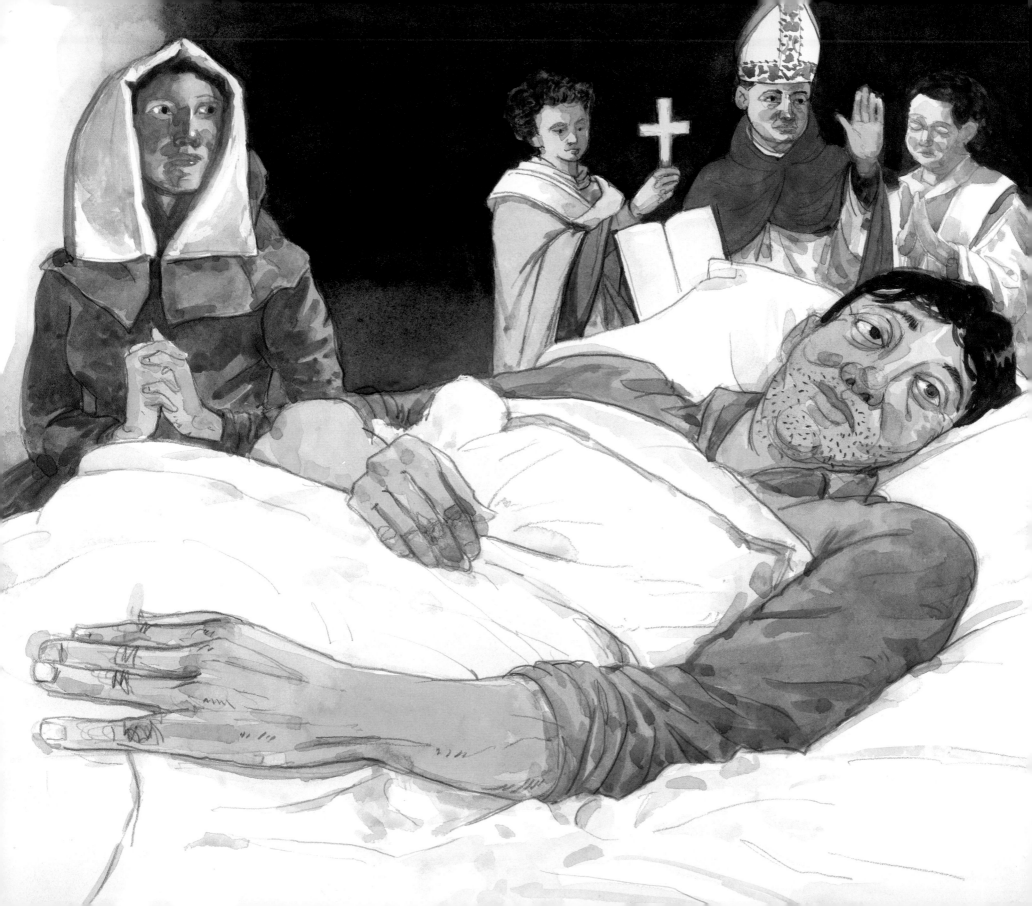

BAD GERMS

make it hard for people to remember
all the good that many of us do, but

GOOD GERMS

help in ways you wouldn't believe.
We just don't go around bragging
about it.

For example, all those leaves that hang around in fall no matter how many times you rake? We are the cleanup crew. We settle on the dead leaves and then get to work, breaking them down by taking what we need and leaving your lawn packed with nutrients to grow grass and other plants in the spring.

How about that funny sound you sometimes hear in your belly when you're hungry? It's not your "stomach growling"—it's us germs breaking down the food! It can get a little noisy at times, but we are hard at work, helping you digest the spaghetti and meatballs you just ate.

And the GOOD germ chefs of the family help to create some of the world's finest foods:

YEAST makes PIZZA DOUGH, MOLD makes CHEESE STICKS, and BACTERIA make the YOGURT you pack in your lunches.

So remember, the next time you sneeze or get a tickle in your throat, think of us working around the clock fighting, defending, infecting, multiplying. For you. For us. Forever.

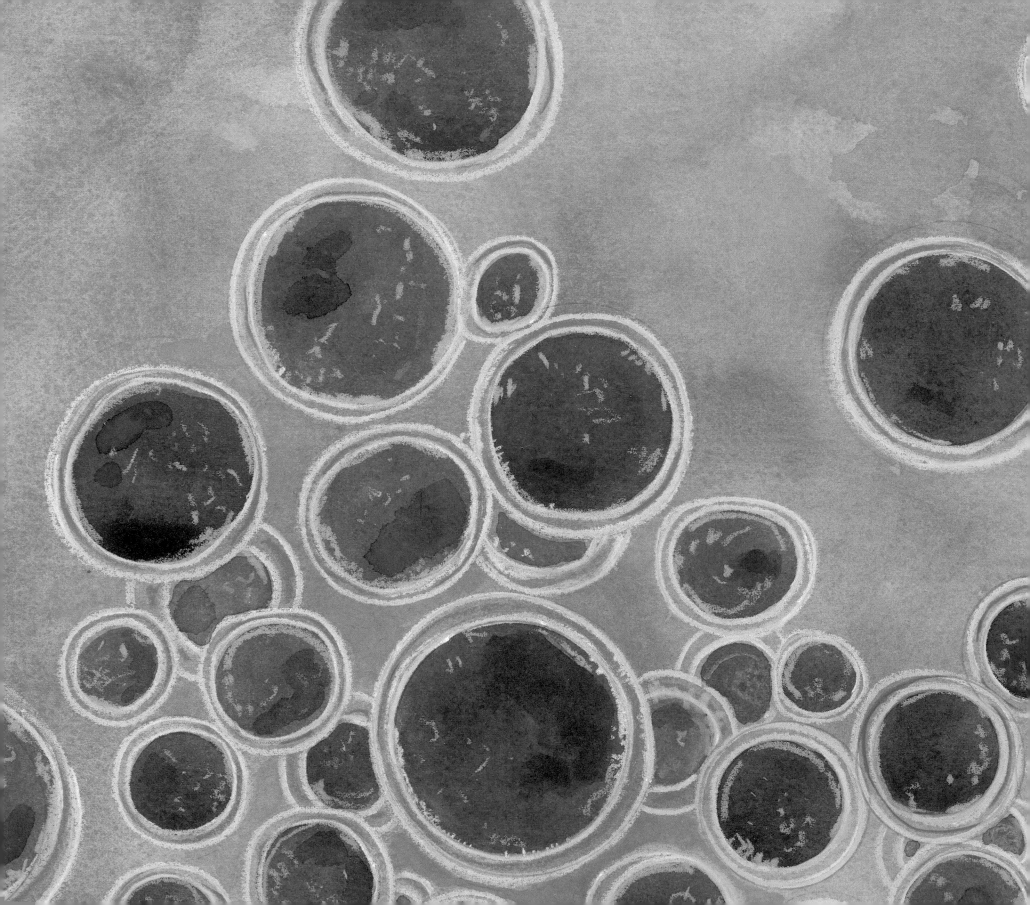

THINGS YOU SHOULD KNOW ABOUT GERMS
THE GOOD, THE BAD, AND THE UGLY

We can't avoid coming in contact with harmful germs in everyday life, but one of the most important things we can do to protect ourselves is also one of the simplest: *hand washing.* I know, you've heard all this before, but it really does work. Water, soap, and vigorous scrubbing for at least thirty seconds help prevent harmful germs from surviving on their favorite carriers—the hands and skin—and minimize the spread of illness.

One of the most startling discoveries in my research of germs was that many illnesses and deaths could have been prevented by simple hand washing. There was a time in history when bathing was thought to cause illness because it allowed "bad air" to enter the body through the uncovered pores of an unclothed person. In the 1400s, Queen Isabella of Spain bragged that she had bathed only two times in her life—when she was born and before her wedding day.

Remember, not all germs are bad. Harmless germs live throughout our bodies, helping to digest food and protecting us from more harmful invaders. Good bacteria boost our immune system so that it can begin fighting whenever a bad germ enters our bodies. The next time that germ appears, your system "remembers" what to do to fight it off.

My inspiration for writing *Germs* came from constantly reminding my children to wash their hands, a task they rarely performed without prodding. I wanted to tell my kids (and everyone else's) how germs make us sick and keep us healthy, and about the myriad ways we battle germs daily. I didn't want to use scare tactics . . . well, maybe a little—but just enough to get them to *wash their hands!*

Our wonderful pediatrician, Dr. David Fenner, echoes much of my research when he warns against overprescribing antibiotics. While antibiotics kill harmful bacteria, they can also kill or weaken the good germs that help us fight viruses. Overprescribing has also led to the rise of "superbugs" that are resistant to some antibiotics. A healthy diet is as important as exercise to build a strong immune system that can keep colds and infections at bay.

Did my kids ever learn to wash their hands? Well, it is still a work in progress. But we did discover an amazing world of microscopic creatures that hugely impact our lives.

GERM TERMS

ACIDOPHILUS—A bacteria that exists naturally in the body and prevents the growth of other harmful bacteria.

ANTIBACTERIAL—Anything that attacks bacteria. Some of the more popular products we use today to fight bacteria are chlorine bleach and alcohol, which is in hand sanitizers.

BACTERIA—Single-celled microscopic organisms that can be shaped like round balls, straight rods, or spirals. They are found everywhere on earth, even inside the human body. Some bacteria are salmonella, E. coli, staphylococcus, and streptococcus.

BLACK DEATH—Also called the plague, this disease is caused by bacteria found in rodents and their fleas. When it spread throughout Europe and the Mediterranean between 1348 and 1350, it is estimated to have killed nearly a third of Europe's population. It's called the black death because black spots would appear on the skin.

E. COLI—Short for the bacteria *Escherichia coli*, most strains are harmless, though others can cause food poisoning. It is named after the German pediatrician Theodor Escherich, who first discovered the bacteria in 1885 in the stools of newborns.

FUNGI—A group of organisms, including molds, yeasts, and mushrooms, that performs a host of functions: fungi break down dead organic matter, serve as a food source, help create medicines, cause diseases, and balance ecosystems.

GERMS—Any microscopic organism that can cause illness. The major types are bacteria, viruses, fungi, and protozoa.

INFLUENZA—Better known as the flu, this contagious viral respiratory illness causes fever, body aches, and coughing, among other symptoms. Serious cases can result in hospitalization and death.

ANTONI VAN LEEUWENHOEK—An amateur scientist from Holland who built his own microscope and was the first to view the tiny living creatures we now call germs.

PASTEURIZATION—A method invented in the 1860s by the French scientist Louis Pasteur that uses heat to kill harmful germs in beverages such as milk.

PENICILLIN—Scottish bacteriologist Alexander Fleming accidentally discovered the bacteria-killing properties of *Penicillium notatum* mold in 1928 while growing a colony of *Staphylococcus aureus* in petri dishes. He earned the Nobel Prize in Physiology or Medicine in 1945. Today penicillin (also known as an antibiotic) saves countless lives each year.

SALMONELLA—A type of bacteria that thrives everywhere and can cause food poisoning, typhoid fever, and blood poisoning. Most infections are contracted by eating or drinking contaminated food or beverages.

SCARLET FEVER—Caused by group A *Streptococcus* bacteria, this disease involves fever, a sore throat, a strawberry-colored tongue, and a scarlet rash.

STAPHYLOCOCCUS AUREUS—Staph is a type of bacteria that can live dormant on our skin and in our nostrils. When the body's defenses are weakened, or when the bacteria enter the body more deeply, it can lead to life-threatening illness resistant to many antibiotics.

STREPTOCOCCUS—Strep includes two types of bacteria. Group A strep commonly causes skin and throat infections. Group B strep can cause serious illness if passed from a mother to a newborn baby.

VACCINATION—Weakened or dead microscopic organisms given to a patient that stimulate the immune system to create protection against a disease.

YELLOW FEVER—Considered one of the most dangerous diseases in the nineteenth century. It is caused by a virus transmitted by mosquitoes and damages the liver, which makes the skin jaundiced, or yellow.

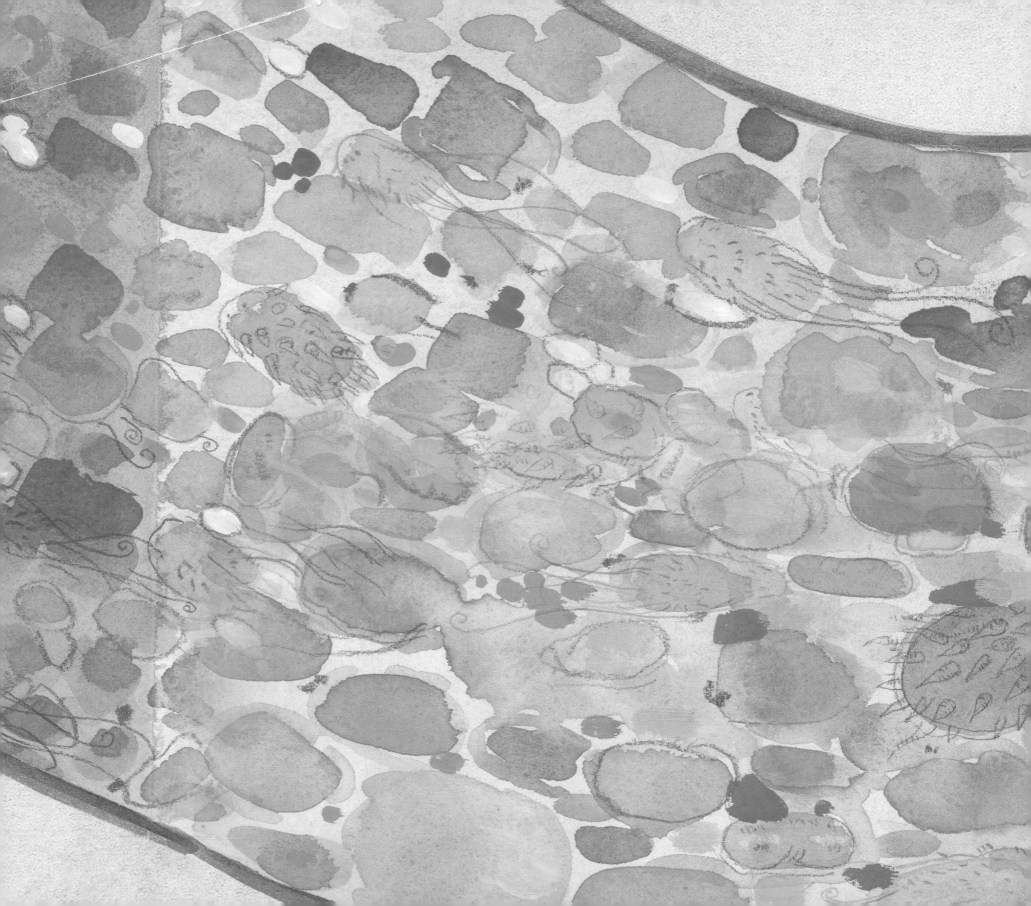